"Last
Hous

Acres. We were warmly greeted, and invited to have a big lunch with forty or so people in this community village who were having a potato-digging bee. After lunch there was a short spiritual reading and then the people dispersed back to work in the field. We were touched by a deep peace of God's love with this community. We were impressed how this community village is also quite self-sufficient. The tour was very enjoyable…

"When we were ready to depart from St. Benedict's Acres I stopped to take a view of the whole farm once more. The women were canning tomatoes and the men were working in the potato field. Cattle, sheep, and the three horses not working in the potato field were grazing. The autumn day gave a colored glory to the trees off on the distant hills, the warmth shared from the people was very easy to sense and the cross on the peak of the hill gave me a peaceful feeling of how we can work the land in harmony. My father made the comment, 'I see nothing but good for helping people here.'"

—Ruth Freeman
The Draft Horse Connection

Apostolic

Farming

Healing the Earth

Catherine Doherty

MADONNA HOUSE PUBLICATIONS

Published by Madonna House Publications
2888 Dafoe Rd
Combermere ON K0J 1L0

www.madonnahouse.org/publications

Expanded Second Edition

Third printing, July 2023

Design by Rob Huston

Canadian Cataloguing in Publication Data

Doherty, Catherine de Hueck, 1896-1985
    Apostolic farming: healing the earth
ISBN 978-0-921440-03-1

    1. Agriculture — Religious aspects — Christianity.
I. Title.
S523.D64 1991   630'.8'82   C91-090260-7

Printed in Canada

To all past, present and future
who will serve at St. Benedict's Acres,
the Madonna House farm.

Contents

Contents

Introduction

Catherine Doherty is foundress of a community of lay men, women, and priests, united in Jesus Christ and in Gospel love. The headquarters and training centre of the community, called Madonna House, are located in the rural village of Combermere, Ontario, Canada. The members staff mission houses throughout the world.

Their works include providing food, clothing, and other basic necessities for those in need; friendship and intercessory prayer; creating beauty through music, drama, arts and crafts; evangelizing through the media; promoting Christian family life; providing year-round spiritual formation to working guests; and farming as apostles, witnessing to the sanctity of creation. Madonna House is a mendicant community, whose works are supported by donations; members do not receive salaries.

Following a two-year period of formation, members make a lifetime commitment; they lead a consecrated life and all are celibates. The community was founded in 1947. Catherine Doherty was a Russian noblewoman, a refugee of the 1917 communist revolution, who founded Friendship Houses prior to founding Madonna House. She died in 1985.

In this expanded second edition of *Apostolic Farming*, a third section has been added: excerpts from writings and interviews of several of the men who have farmed the Madonna House land and who have been formed by Catherine's teaching.

Part One

Memories of a Russian Farm

It doesn't do to make the earth angry

The stocky peasant with the square beard that tumbled down to the middle of his chest stood easily before my father. I heard his usually calm voice acquire a vehement accent: "No, sir," he said, "it doesn't do to make the earth angry. It will punish us if we do."

The words struck me forcibly. I was around thirteen. I wanted to know what our farm manager meant by this strange sentence, and asked my father that night. He smiled; then his face became serious. Father explained to me quietly and with a depth of feeling I did not suspect he had, that mankind was the child and servant of the earth. The earth was our mother, in a manner of speaking, and farming was a holy way of life. It was a way of life that God meant for the majority of people. In the growing of things, first to feed one's own family, and then to serve one's neighbor, man fulfiled himself as a workman.

He went on to say that work was not a curse. Adam had worked; God himself had worked. Work was holy, especially work on and with the earth. One had to be reverent when one was a farmer. God spoke very clearly to those who farmed and taught them many lessons in this place of formation. Above all, He taught them prayer, faith, humble submission to his most holy will, and reverence for all created things—trees, flowers, seeds, grains, animals. Even the tools used for this tending of the earth and of living things must be reverenced.

All this I remembered recently as I discussed our farm with others who were interested in the land. We sat up late talking about chores and about ways of working the earth and fertilizing it. When I returned to my little cabin I couldn't sleep for hours. Out of a distant past a thousand images crowded into my mind. They filled my heart with a strange sadness. Long-forgotten pictures, sounds, and smells overwhelmed me. I began to recognize something that had been bewildering me and strangely hurting me since I first came to this new world. Like a refrain to all these memories, a phrase kept intruding itself—"this beautiful land, this beautiful land." Yes, it was becoming clear; this infinitely rich and gracious earth of the new world was being ruined and destroyed by man.

You must put back what you take away

The spade-bearded figure of our farm superintendent of yesteryear rose before me. He was discussing a field with my father, who had a farm of 800 arable acres which had been in our family since the twelfth century. He was talking to my father about one field in particular. He said it was sick.

One unacquainted with the Russian peasant farmer's speech would have thought that he was talking of a person. As he explained, the earth was black and soft to the touch. It looked healthy but it was not well. Oh no, it was very sick! He advised my father to let it rest, to let it sleep its sickness out.

He told my father why this field got sick. It was because we had not put back into it what we had taken away from it. It had grown wheat last year, but there was a new hired man who hadn't put the straw back

15

after the harvest. Earnestly, the peasant—the farm doctor—kept repeating that the law of soil fertility was very simple: you must put back what you take away.

The earth never hurries

I recall the spade-bearded man discussing with my father another field that he said was dying. Sleep, he said, would not restore that field. It had to be healed lovingly and patiently. He spoke of trees as the remedy.

They decided on a mixture of evergreens and deciduous trees. Planting only evergreen trees would make the soil sour; leaves from deciduous trees were needed to feed the earth over long years.

I asked my father why he was giving so much acreage to trees which grew very slowly. "The earth never hurries," he said, "and if a man makes her ill he has to apologize to her, beg her forgiveness, and start all over again to make her well and fruitful. Sometimes it takes four generations to restore the soil that has been hurt by one generation."

Father told me that once upon a time a large part of our land had been very sick. My great-great grandfather decided that the only way to restore it to health was to plant it with trees, and this he did. He left instructions for his great-grandson (my grandfather) to cut down the trees and plow the land when the latter's son (my father) would turn six years old. Father remembered men cutting down those mighty trees and plowing the earth. It was black again and rich and full of life. It was, in my day, our most fertile piece of earth.

Farmers' gold

I remember thrashing time. In a structure that had a hard oak floor with a roof over it, but no walls, men with flails hit the grain and sang to the rhythm of their flails. The wind blew the chaff and the straw away, and it would be lightly plowed back into the soil, thus giving something back to the land for what it had given us. Sometimes in the fall and the spring, they would plow in some dark, heavy manure which the peasant called "farmers' gold." They also brought to the field rich earth from the forest and sometimes muck from the marshes, mixed with plants that grew there.

Maybe I'm very unscientific, but I dread to see dead chemicals go into the earth. I dread to see vegetables, grains, berries, and trees fed these chemicals, for even one season. It reminds me of babies fed on formulas and bottles, and denied the rich sweet milk of their own mothers. But in this, our new world, men are not afraid to feed the earth's children crops produced with inert, lifeless matter of their own making.

We also had thirty-six cows in the milking barn. Cows that were dry had their own barn. There was a third barn for cows with calves, and next to this was my favourite place, where the calves were separated from their mothers. I liked to play with them there.

The green road

How far away those days seem now! The barns were solidly built, with good big logs. They had earthen floors which were hard as rocks. The golden straw was changed often. The stalls had been polished and worn through centuries of cleaning and use by the people who worked there and the animals which were kept there.

Every morning the man in charge would drop sweet-smelling hay into those stalls. And then the cows would get a ration of greens which used to come from what mother called the "green road."

This green road was a simple thing. We had acres of beets, turnips, and other root vegetables. All the greens from these, and the short rich grass that was cut from around the house, weedings from the gardens and the orchards, plus other green stuff that grows in summer—all this was laid behind the barn and it made a sort of road, the "green road." The snow would fall on this and pack it down. Then hired men would cut through this strange mass and bring it to the animals for a change of diet. The beasts loved it.

I can still smell the bitter-sweet odor of burning wood under one of the strangest contraptions I have ever seen. It was a huge vat, or round cauldron, firmly imbedded in a cone-like structure of stones and cement, with a place to put wood underneath. A tousled-haired boy was always in attendance in the morning, boiling the magic potion in the vat, and adding dry, clean logs to the fire.

Into this vat went all the household compost matter—potato peelings and such. Salt was added, and water, and the boy had a huge stick with which he mixed this mess. By noon the cooking was done and the mixture cooled and given to the milking cows. This was their dessert!

In my native language I don't think there is a word equivalent to the English word "chore", which seems to connote something heavy, done reluctantly, for pay. Work with animals and the land was never a chore for us but a way of life. Perhaps it seems funny that a woman would say, "I've got to go and relieve my beauties of their burden." She was speaking, of course, about milking the cows—but her language showed that she loved her work. There was a great love of animals and a gentleness in handling them.

Granny used to say, "An unloved cow will be a dry cow."

I had never seen feed or fertilizer in bags

It dawned on me that, in my experience of farming in Russia, I had never seen feed in bags. We had about two-hundred chickens, fifty ducks, seventy-five turkeys, and forty geese. I had never seen our flocks spend a whole summer imprisoned in a scientifically built poultry house, nor had I seen them fed any kind of scientifically packaged feed. (Neither had I seen fertilizer come in bags.)

The poultry were fed on golden wheat, greyish-yellow oats, and brownish-black buckwheat seeds. They were let loose in a field of grass. They had their houses, to which they returned at night and where they laid their eggs. Maybe it is distance and time that make me remember them as a happy flock, a very contented bunch of birds. They cackled their lives away and did what God meant them to do—wax fat and give us eggs, feathers, and their meat.

Serenity and peace in being one with nature

We didn't have many fences in Russia. I presume it would have cost a fortune to fence in a thousand-acre farm. But we had shepherds and shepherdesses. The cows, horses, and sheep, all had their shepherds. Some were barely out of childhood; others were old men and women. They knew the serenity and peace that comes from living a life of silence and being one with nature and nature's God. All were deeply religious, and the villagers considered even the young ones wise. They were respected, and they loved their work.

These people were also experts in whittling, spinning, and all kinds of creative work that today are considered hobbies. Some of them were musicians, especially the men. They made flutes out of reeds. The reeds made beautiful tunes.

I remember an old shepherd who used to come and play his tunes in the kitchen. When I asked him where he got his tunes from, he answered, "From the wind and the trees and the song of the grass. From the talk of the flowers and the song of the brooks."

Are we eating the fruits of the earth, or are we eating chemicals?

I do not know much about modern scientific farming. Combines frighten me by their sheer immensity. I can feel the earth weep under their heavy treads. It seems to me that they take from the earth but give nothing in return. Horses, as they go a-plowing, fertilize the earth. Man's hand is gentle when he tills the soil. There is a less hurried pace about the whole thing. Tractors have a frantic pace about them. I cannot understand this hurry to get returns and results.

Today in our new world the earth is treated as if it were a factory. It is wounded by machines. Chemicals are sprayed, from airplanes and by tractors, onto the earth, the fruits, vegetables, and flowers. The earth is fed man-made chemicals that produce a large but far less healthy or tasty crop. Farming has become almost a synthetic factory with a production line. Are we eating the fruits of the earth, or are we eating chemicals that God never meant us to eat?

And what about all the insects that get killed in the process? We used to have a reverence for bees. Every farmer was a beekeeper. But I have seen apiaries destroyed in a single summer in this wondrous land of ours by some new spray invented by some learned man somewhere—probably someone far away from a farm who never had the privilege of working with things that grow, nor with insects which God created to help things grow.

Prayerfully, everybody went to work

I remember, in the old days of Russia, that a rust came upon the grain. No one was in a hurry to invent something to spray it with. Prayerfully, everybody went to work, following the laws of nature, trying to grow a rust-proof wheat. I'm not sure, but I think Russia succeeded. Long trial and error methods of cross-breeding brought it into being.

Today man makes profit out of the soil, which is all he seems to care about. Yes, farms are becoming, not the pride and livelihood of a family, but the investment of absentee landlords who have never lived personally with the gentle cycle of nature. But this state of affairs will not last long. One day the earth, our mother, will become devastated. Farming may be business, even big business, but people who forget it is a way of life will someday weep over their forgetfulness.

I can still hear the soft voice of the old Russian peasant when he responded to my question as to how he knew so much about the earth. I can see the smile forming on his lips as he bent his great height towards me and replied, "Little lady, of course I know about the earth, and you will too. I came from her and I will return to her. Dust to dust! That's the way God decreed we should come from Him into the world. That is how we shall go back to Him. He has placed our soul into this house of sod, and from the soil He will receive it back."

In Russia the farmer was called *Krestianin*, which simply means "Christian"; and Russians had the right idea, because a farmer should be the epitome of a Christian. This way of naming the farmer is a sort of christianization of the world through farming. It's beautiful.

Part Two

Towards an Apostolic Farm

Part Two

Towards an Appetite for Land

Our farm: a dream dreamt in God

We have a farm here at Madonna House called St. Benedict's Acres. This farm was born out of a dream of mine. When I say "dream," I mean thoughts that pass back and forth from my heart to my mind and then return back to my heart, to lie there quietly until the hand of God touches them and revives them, and brings them forth for me to pray about. Then the cycle from the heart to the mind and back begins again. I call these my "dreams dreamt in the Lord," because they are for his purposes.

When I say I dream in the Lord and for the Lord, I simply mean that I dream of serving God in others. To me, whoever is in love with God must incarnate or live out their love immediately. Jesus Christ, the Second Person of the Holy Trinity, became man out of love for us. He said, "I have come to serve," and I must imitate him in service.

Perhaps this preliminary introduction was unnecessary, but I wanted to put it on paper so that the sustenance of such dreams becomes clear to anyone who reads this story of our farm.

I had also dreamt about our Handicraft Centre, and I dreamt about our Mission Gift Shop. I dreamt about a mountain on which these would be placed. I dreamt of artists coming to us, and scholars. Lo and behold, all these dreams have come true! We have scholars and artists amongst us now.

But long before I dreamt about these, I dreamt about a farm. In my earlier years of serving the poor in our Friendship Houses, both in the steaming streets of Harlem and in the cold and windy streets of Toronto slums, my mind would fly away to my native land and to our farms there. I would think of the simple, time-honored ways they were worked, and of the good tiredness that came to all of us who worked on such farms. Some of these memories I have just shared with you. Yes, lots of things came back to me, but I asked myself from whence or where I would ever get a farm. However, the Lord of Hosts has a way of making dreams come true.

First, a subsistence situation

I remember when we moved to Combermere, in rural Ontario. Before my arrival on May 17, 1947, I had ordered some seedling apple trees for planting and they came by mail a few days before our arrival. I had also asked a neighbor to plow and fertilize with manure a part of our small acreage there, so that we could use it for gardening. Even while on our way from Chicago to Combermere, I was planning a mini-farm that would include a few chickens, a pig, a vegetable garden, the beginnings of an orchard, and some flowers and bees.

All this was accomplished between the years 1947 and 1950. I had two bee hives in what is today our orchard. The apple trees grew well there, if slowly, and St. Joseph's Garden was full of radishes, lettuce, peas, beans, potatoes, cucumbers, and even a patch of strawberries. In another corner I planted asparagus, red currants, black currants, and some raspberries.

It was far from being a farm, and was rather a subsistence situation, for we had very little money; the eggs came in handy, and so did the chickens, for meat, when they got older. I did have fun doing it.

Years passed by. The dream of a real farm was wrapped up and laid aside in my heart, waiting for the hand of God to touch it; and so He did one day.

The dream begins to come true

The first man with farming experience to arrive was Ronnie MacDonell, in 1955. But we had no farm. A friend, Baron José de Vinck, had purchased in the meantime what was known as "Ruddy's farm," located just a mile from us. He allowed us to use the arable part of the land, such as it was, for gardening, and we purchased a few milk cows. Ronnie, who was the only farmer at Madonna House, took over and taught quite a few others on that acreage. But the chickens, pigs, and bees were still on the property of Madonna House itself.

One day a neighbor arrived, a man who dabbled in local real estate, and he told me that what I needed was a farm. Inwardly I immediately responded, but outwardly I was very quiet, and explained to him that I couldn't possibly raise money for any high-priced farm. He said he wanted to sell me Kelly's farm, about six miles down the road. I had known Mr. Kelly, and had nursed him on that farm. I would get there in the winter on my sleigh, for I used to go nursing by sleigh quite often. I remembered going up the hill to his house which, since he was sick and lived alone, I used to clean for him on my nursing visits. He had been an extraordinary man, this Mr. Kelly. Even into his seventies he would still walk from that farm to the church, a good five or six miles, and walk back again. He was one of the rugged people who lived in the area.

The idea of purchasing his farm touched something in my heart, and so Ronnie, Father John Callahan (our chaplain), and I went with the real estate agent to look it over. It was a farm of about 350 acres. Mr. Kelly had planted some grain, and there was forage for the cows. It looked good to us and the price was around $5,600. As I prayed while looking at the farm, something told me that this was *it*—the beginning of this dream of mine coming true, by the grace of God.

Would you believe it, in less than two years the $6,000 was paid, and we took this as a sign that God wanted us to have this farm. It was born very humbly and simply, in blood, sweat, and tears, but also with much beauty; and in endless discussions, with much frustration, and through great perseverance.

Ronnie MacDonell donated a tractor. We brought the cows over from the borrowed farmland, and eventually the pigs and hens from Madonna House. The vegetables and berries were also transferred to the farm.

Towards an Apostolic Farm

Let us step back for a moment and look at the farm as I saw it in my heart and mind. A farm can be looked at from a hundred angles, but I always looked at it from an apostolic angle, and I saw our farm as doing apostolic farming.

Why? Because the word "apostle" means one who is sent on a special mission, and is usually applied to one sent to bring the Good News of Jesus Christ. Let us stop here for a moment and reflect.

What were the greatest tidings that the world has ever heard? Aren't they heard in the cry of a little Child who became man while He was God and who gave us truth? To put it in a scriptural way: the Word of God leapt down from his throne in heaven (*Wisdom 18:15*), became incarnate and walked amongst us. God's only Son was born unto us and He gave us himself and the gospel of love.

So in my mind anything connected with being apostolic is connected with Jesus Christ, who is charity. Charity is another name for love, and where love is, God is—for God is love.

When we approach farming, when we add the word "apostolic" to the word "farming," we simply mean we are engaged in farming because we want to spread the Good News by bringing God to everyone who sees or hears of our farm. We bring the Good News by living the gospel, and there is no better place to live the gospel than on a farm.

Close to God in the country

When one thinks about it, Jesus was born in the countryside and lived there most of his lifetime. He wasn't a farmer, but his gospel is filled with examples from farming. He talked about vineyards and crops, about grain and seeds and plowing. He used stories about farming and chose examples taken from nature, which the farmer handles constantly.

Nowhere do men and women come closer to God than in the country, in the rural areas, and nowhere are they closer to Him than when they till the earth and look after the flock. How Christ loved to use the parables of sheep and shepherd, and of all kinds of flocks. Tenderness to animals, to the earth and all growing things was in his voice. Have we that tenderness? Have we that love and understanding?

To bring the Good News it is not enough for a farmer to train as an apostle. One must integrate apostolic knowledge and the love in one's heart into every day actions. Again my mind turns to Him who gave us the Good News which made us apostles, to the One who sent us to be his apostles.

Well, have you wanted for anything?

We notice that Christ walked in poverty, that He sent his disciples without staffs, without gold or silver, even without shoes. They departed full of doubts, even as we would have. If we listen well to the gospel stories, we will sense a teasing quality in his voice when, upon their return from their mission, He asked them, "Well? Have you wanted for anything?" They were compelled to reply that they had not wanted for anything! I envision the farmers of Madonna House to exemplify Christ as they go about the art of farming.

They are men who try to live gospel poverty, who delight in making do, or in making things. There is so much joy in doing something yourself instead of having some impersonal machine do it for you.

The apostolic farmer is a man of creativity and can, when the need arises (as poverty so often makes it arise), create something to lighten his burden or to help the growth of his works. That is why those who work on our farm try very hard to get additional knowledge of how to weld and to repair things.

We are but God's stewards

We work our farm with God's money, for every cent that has gone into this farm of ours, which we call St. Benedict's Acres, was donated to us in charity. We are custodians of every cent that is given to us—we are but God's stewards. Our custodianship and our stewardship must be exceedingly thorough and holy.

Fundamentally, like most farmers of this district, we got ourselves a poor farm. It isn't bad that we started with a poor farm, for it made us so much more one with our neighbors. It's true that in one fell swoop you could pour thousands of dollars into a farm, buy all the machinery, buy fertilizer and so on, and even with our poor soil you would have a luxurious farm that no farmer around here or in most parts of the world would dare dream of. But since we want to identify with the poor, we are glad we had a poor farm to start working.

I see the apostolic farmer as one who seeks to make a farm richly productive by using the simplest means and the least possible amount of money; who feeds his brothers and sisters at the least possible expense, so that the money saved might go to other places who need it.

Love that spills itself into the earth

Apostolic farming stems from love and is ingenious, creating something out of nothing. It studies how to do a thing more cheaply. Land, animals, tools, and machinery are all seen as holy things and as immensely valuable, inspiring awe at God's bounty to us.

I visualize farming as being a witness to love, so that people may come and ask how it is possible that we farm without much money. My answer would be, "Anybody can farm with money, but an apostle farms with prayer and with love that spills itself into the earth, cherishing and working it, getting the best out of it without harming it, and loving it as God loved it."

He gazes at the earth reverently, knowing that God created it and that it is beloved by God. As I said, Jesus Christ was very close to the earth. He slept on it and used its images for his stories. But before that, God— the Triune God—created it and populated it and made all living things grow.

Yes, apostolic farming must be love that spills itself onto the earth. It is a very slow process and it teaches farmers lessons that cannot be learned from books. It strips them naked of pre-conceived notions and makes them whole persons again. He who works with the earth from whence he came and to which he will return gets healed of his wounds. He becomes deeply reconciled with God, and walks with Him at eventide while they both look over the creation of their hands.

Why do we farm?

When I am asked why we farm, the answer comes very easily: because we have to eat! There are a great multitude of us in Madonna House who have to be fed, and the simplest way is to work to produce our food. Work by the sweat of our brows, as we are supposed to, and produce it in the best and cheapest way we know how.

So our first reason for farming is seemingly utilitarian: to provide food for the growing family that God sends us. This also embodies the spirit of followers of Christ. It brings us face to face with the fact that we are poor, that we have to work for the things we need or do without them, as much as we can. The providence that our farmers must manifest is based on the providence of God.

Our second aim is to learn to farm so that we can go to the furthest end of the earth and produce food for adults and children who have never known, for even one day of their life, freedom from the pangs of hunger.

Yes, the real reason for apostolic farming is to express love of one's neighbor, and it has two means toward this end: feeding and teaching. These the farmer utilizes by loving the earth and loving the work he does. He learns what the best food is and how to grow it. He delights in gospel poverty and simplicity, in producing all that is needed for the family at the lowest price, yet for greatest health.

Our farm is a sort of training centre

The depths of a farmer's love for his fellowmen and for the earth is exemplified by ingenuity, which may be expressed through trial and error. It is difficult to explain but I see it this way: today we learn at our farm; tomorrow we are in some country where we don't have a tractor, a horse, or a plow. We have just two hands and primitive tools.

When we go there we will already have a basic, fundamental knowledge of the things that have to be done. At first we will slowly do things the way the local people do them. Shoulder to shoulder with them, we use those primitive tools if need be, or stand deep in water growing rice, or deep in sand in the Sahara. Here again, ingenuity is accompanied by great respect for the people we are working with, and by deep concentration and observation. Later we might introduce some of our ways, but very gently, with simple means, like making a plow in a black-smith shop and getting the wood for it from a nearby forest, being careful not to offend or to "show off."

I see the farmer as a man of learning, yet of unlearning; of trial and error, and of fortitude and courage. I see him as a man standing up, ready to go and bring to others the knowledge he has gained by the sweat of his brow, and the sweat of his soul, in our little corner of Canada. He aims to bring the Good News to everyone he meets.

Sitting at the feet of elders

Apostolic farming goes deep. It doesn't keep to itself. It doesn't only use its better-educated brain. It humbly goes to the elders of the village, and to farmers who have been farming for many years but are not yet elders. We

43

sit at their feet, as it were, and listen, gently, courteously, respectfully, for they have the knowledge of centuries behind them. Some part of that knowledge will be useful. We can discuss it and appraise it in the light of new discoveries, and it can become something very valuable in our hands.

We use the intelligence that God has given us to deeply research things that deal with farming. Incidentally, research is also a means of communicating the Glad News to the people with whom one comes in contact through research.

It is tragic for farmers to have a closed mind, to think that there is only one way of doing a thing, to argue in order to get their own way, or not to be able to say, "I don't know" or "I am wrong—let's try it another way. Maybe their way is the right way."

It takes courage to endure trial and error constantly, to face endless small failures (realizing that failures are stepping stones to success), to remember that one must be ready to start all over again at every moment, with God's help.

So much depends on this alertness of love

Apostolic farmers need a constant inner alertness that amounts to walking the furrow with God. Being in love with God, they are so aware of the sanctity of his creatures that they are alert to everything. Much depends on this alertness of love, on this self-forgetfulness, on this not being preoccupied with one's problems. Alertness goes hand in hand with this prayer: "Lord, teach me to show your face to those who live around me, through ordinary things."

A farmer can't be self-centered; he has too many people and too many things depending on him. He has too big a job to be concerned with himself. For the creatures of God with which the farm deals, both plants and animals as well as the people it feeds, need his constant attention.

He gradually develops real knowledge, experimental knowledge, in which book knowledge has been weighed, tried, changed, adapted or accepted. Slowly he grows in ability to feed his brothers and sisters.

This requires vision, and lack of fear. It requires the ability to take the rap. It requires maturity of mind and heart, namely, love. We Christians are called to show the face of God in little things, in growing plants and young animals, making them produce what they must, in order to feed others.

Holy poverty should be a constant meditation

Holy poverty should be a constant meditation. We must continually ask ourselves, "How can I do without this? How can I substitute something less expensive?" For if we are slowly acquiring the reputation of having what is unaffordable to most people, how can we show the face of God to the poor?

I confess that it disturbs me that, to take a small example, we follow a textbook which says we have to keep chickens in a coop all year round and we are to pour into those chickens a tremendous amount of commercial feed. If we had ingenuity, we would simply buy a flock and let them run loose like the farmers used to do. We would find out if it is possible to substitute their feed with something less expensive, and compare the results with the book. I understand that today we have begun to grow grains to feed the chickens, which will reduce our feed bills tremendously.

We seem to be moving toward having immense farm buildings, with everything just so. This is unfortunate, and I question if it is inescapable or inevitable. Somewhere, some place in my heart, I have a pain, because I think we are not using enough ingenuity of love to reduce our expenditures to level with those of people around us. What will happen if we have every convenience here and then are sent to the missions to farm without any conveniences?

Answers can be found

We talk a lot and we subscribe to an awful lot of half-truths, based on book learning.

But I could visualize one of our men going to a university, taking the entire four-year course in agriculture, and then throwing the whole thing out, so to speak, and starting again with a basic recipe he has learned at the feet of humble and simple farmers.

It is good for us to go to agricultural colleges, but when we go there let's ask questions like the following: "Sir, how would you have run a farm a hundred years ago in Canada? How would you run a farm if you didn't have any money for a tractor or for fertilizer?"

Answers can be found, but we must pray over each answer to make it fruitful and applicable to us here and now. The knowledge that an apostolic farmer gleans, like a bee, from everywhere must be prayed over and experimented with.

We must offer ourselves to God by saying, "Lord, I have been to far away places, even if only by mail. I haven't been idle. I have tried to put thoughts of myself away. I have sought your face in nature, in animals, in the earth, and in my brothers. Now let me be grist to your mill and make me into a hard grain so that I will make good flour." An apostolic farmer makes of himself bread, so as to feed others, even as he is fed daily on the Eternal Bread—the wheat for which he has grown himself.

Great humility

There was a time when many people thought that farming was menial work and "beneath" them. This is not so, because every action has eternal value. Tossing garbage cans and manure around have the same value as writing a thesis or working at any other occupation that appears to be cleaner. There is nothing dirty about farming. Everything the farmer deals with is clean and everything has a purpose. The manure is going to help give us food for next year. The hog will be eaten. The cow will produce calves and give milk and meat. Everything on the farm leads to the feeding of mankind. How can farming be dirty when it feeds the temple of God, as St. Paul calls our body, and allows Christ to come and dwell in that temple?

Farming must be approached with great humility. The learned man, the really learned one, is aware that he knows very little. The apostolic farmer has for his teacher God and the nature God has created. He learns at the source of all schooling, where everything began, where all knowledge originally comes from. He is reverent of the school of nature and its experience, and isn't afraid of it.

However learned, he never shows his learning to others with words puffed up with pride. He uses humble similes, like the parables of Christ; he has the right to do so—he lives them! An apostolic farmer is understanding of others because he is understood by God and contemplates him in the mystery of life in the country.

A whole world to save... by feeding the pigs

The desire for a purifying way of life still sometimes knocks at the heart of a man. Opportunities for this are all there on the farm, provided that one sees them for what they are. But if a daily task is seen as a burdensome chore, forced upon us, as it were, this isn't a Christian approach. The farmer hasn't chores to do; he has a whole world to save by feeding the pigs.

Farming demands the whole of a man. It is a good way to die to self and selfishness, because the demands of nature and animals remind him of his duty of the moment. The goal of feeding one's brothers and sisters is always before him.

The apostolic farmer makes the earth fecund, not only with the fecundity of good farming, but with the fecundity of his own life, so that those who come after him shall truly eat of the fruit of his life.

A farmer is a man who feeds others. How can one preach Christ to people who have an empty stomach? In a manner of speaking, the farmer holds the keys to the preaching of Christ and in this humble way he will be our forerunner. Those of us who may go to missions will have been given the keys to the preaching of the gospel by our farmers, especially today—when half the world is hungry.

Tomorrow they will be our leaders

I foresee the time when our farmers will be our leaders and we their followers, because we will be called into the wilderness where they have gone, to hoe the hearts of men and of nature. Tomorrow the apostolic farmer will be the person who knows, and we his obedient servants. He will be the man upon whom the tired, the sick, and the hungry will look as a saviour, and they will call him that in many tongues.

He will thereby be bringing Christ to people and preaching the Good News in a language everybody understands. When a non-Christian of any race beholds our farmer plowing a field, with whatever tool he is using, they will see love of the earth in his gesture. His love for the earth and his love of nature will inspire a love of God.

Yes, it is quite possible that in a not too distant future we might be called to help feed our brothers and sisters in other parts of the world. It is strange that we do not see these things with our eyes, and even more strange that we don't hear them with the ear of our souls.

We must pray for vision

We must pray for vision, for ingenuity; we must get out of the rut of fear, the rut of emotions, and really enter into farming as an apostolate or mission. We must get experimental knowledge and, with very minimal spending, make our farm as productive as if we had poured into it a million dollars. It will take a long time but we will get there with love and prayer. Then we can truthfully say to the Lord, "I have learned to be humble and poor, and an apostle, and now I can go forth and teach those who are poor, even poorer than I am."

The vision of a farmer is unlimited, because he has before him the unlimited horizon of the earth. He goes up a hill and sees more earth, more fields, and more trees, and he remembers that only God can make a tree. Because his vision is unlimited, he can pass on his vision to others who haven't got the privilege of constantly dealing with God's creation.

The tranquillity of God's order

His work habits must be orderly, for how can one help bring order into someone else's life if one can't keep his tools in order? How can he bring order into human hearts and minds if his barn is a mess, his cows are never cured, and the barnyard needs cleaning? How can he offer men the Bread of Life if he neglects his stock or feeds it wrongly? How can he help others come out of the mire of sin if his house is a mire of disorder?

There is a discipline that faces a farmer in maintaining order. He gladly takes this discipline upon himself, because he knows that disorder will immediately be reflected in living things and in human beings.

If he doesn't wash his hands, the cow might get sick, and so might the people who drink the milk of these cows. If he skips a feed or feeds too much or too little, the animals may get sick or die, or his family will suffer from the expenditure of useless money. Disorder can go on and on like a whirlwind. But he understands the tranquillity of God's order, accepts it and shares it.

A farmer walks purposefully

A farmer walks purposefully; he doesn't waste one moment of time, a precious, God-given commodity. If he misses a day, there will be no hay. If he plows a little too late, there will be no harvest. If he seeds one hour too late and a storm comes, then all his work will be undone. He respects time and knows that it makes up seasons and hours. He knows how he must use it, and neither allows it to be his master nor makes it his slave.

The farmer follows its call promptly and joyously, even if it lifts him out of his warm bed early in the morning and brings him back to his warm bed only late at night. He knows it is God's call; he knows that God has given him, like every Christian, a part of eternity in which to grow in love and to become a saint.

A man of integrity

The apostolic farmer is a man of integrity and he deals with things of integrity. There

55

is nothing deceitful about a field. It is honest, straight and clean, for it comes from the hands of God. The farmer touches God in his creation as it came from his hands.

Somewhere along the road of history man began to pollute fields and to rape this planet with his greed and with a technology that is sometimes used to pervert what God had intended for us. Earth and water are defiled with all kinds of things that do not belong in them, and people have become unhealthy, eating junk food and greed-motivated, polluted food products.

A farmer deals with the mystery of life. We were watching a film showing the whole process of growth, and someone remarked that they couldn't understand what happened in that little seed to make it grow. Frankly and simply, what happened was a mystery of God.

Because he touches God all the time in the mystery of nature and so is familiar with Him, a farmer can easily tell others about God. Respectful of himself, of the soil and all growing things, he communes with God and hence can communicate to others this God with whom he relates so easily through everyday work and life.

The apostolic farmer is a man of prayer; he talks to God about the needs of the animals, about the seeds he has to plant. He knows his limitations, and it is on his knees that he begs God for light, for ingenuity, for vision, so that he can produce something out of nothing. For he understands very well that alone he can never do it, but with God all things are possible. It is said that with God, the impossible takes only three minutes longer! The main point is that God has said, "Without Me you can do nothing."

Create something out of nothing

For a moment I digress and recall how amazing it was that during the Russian revolution we really did create something out of nothing. I remember the time when we had no shoes to wear and there was no leather in that part of the world to get a pair of shoes made. It was getting very cold and we were desperate to have something to put on our feet.

Suddenly our eyes fell on some curtains that were hanging on our window and Mother said, "Let's make ourselves shoes out of these velvet curtains." But we couldn't find anything to make soles with. Then our eyes fell on a linoleum-covered kitchen floor. So we took up the linoleum and made ourselves soles, for it didn't seem too important to have linoleum on the floor at the time. We had never before cut out a pair of shoes, but in the end we sure had a wonderful pair of medieval shoes, so that we could go outside.

When we got hungry (and we were very hungry during that revolution for a while), the stuff we ate was, in fact, good to eat, although we wouldn't have eaten it before. Wild nettles, for instance, with hot water poured over them, made good soup, and was something like spinach.

Lord, help me to care for your vineyard

This farmer is a restless creature, for in him is the immense restlessness of God who cries out in his eternal search for souls, "I thirst!" (*John 19:28*) So the farmer is a man of thirst, not for his own opinion but for the opinion of others, everywhere. He searches to find out what people have learned through the centuries, in every part of the world. He seeks that knowledge, and then humbly and reverently brings it all to God, before whom he bows his head and prays, "Lord, help me to care for your vineyard, for the portion that You have given me!"

Yes, he is a man of prayer and a man of dreams, this apostolic farmer. For unless he dreams, he will not go very far. But his dreams must be dreamt in God. He must place all his dreams in God and ask God to make them come true. But he must not dream of making more money to build bigger things or to get more machinery to make his life easier. He must dream of simpler ways so as to make the life of other people easier by using ingenuity as a fruit of his love for others.

We must keep in mind that we are farming to feed not only ourselves, but others. We are farming to learn to feed others under conditions that yesterday we didn't even visualize could exist.

A pilgrimage without leaving his farm

The apostolic farmer is a tireless traveller and seeker, a pilgrim of Christ, searching for more knowledge, searching in places where nobody goes, and using wisely the time when he can get away from the farm. Day by day he is ever alert, seeking far and wide, ways and means to do the impossible a little better and a little faster.

He is a pilgrim of the Absolute, of God, even when his pilgrimaging is in search of a new type of hoe or a way of fertilizing without paying money for the fertilizer. His ingenuity is visible to God, morning, noon and night. He makes a pilgrimage without leaving his farm, because the charity of Christ urges him on.

Deep are the roots of apostolic farming. Its roots, like its fruits, are always God's, and they are fertilized with things of God: death to self and selfishness, gospel poverty and obedience and chastity, wise use of time, and veneration for all creatures.

Farmers mature through listening, silence, and prayer to God the Father; and they can speak to Adam about digging the earth. We have to restore the earth, because God the Father wants it fertile, wants it to be worked by us, wants us to realize what a great privilege is ours.

The fatherhood of God in a farm

I see the fatherhood of God in a farm, in a true and deep, yet ordinary sense. Man is a protector and provider, and on a farm man truly feeds his family by the work of his hands. That is why I feel so deeply that our farming is united with the *agape*, the love feast, of the Mass, for liturgical worship and food go together. The Mass goes together with the work that is being done on the farm. Yet all this is deeper than anything that I can say, for as a farm develops that unity that I dreamt about long ago, the unity of man and God with the earth, the unity of persons, the unity with nature, I am sure you will begin to see wonderment born again in the heart of man.

It is the wonderment of a new life coming in the spring, the wonderment of the beauty of autumn that sheds its leaves to fertilize the earth. Thousands of wonderments come to he who is open to wonder. They come to him by the grace of God and he knows that he must pass these things on to others, to a world that ceases to wonder.

The farm has a very special role: to bring about unity

As we look about us we find little unity. We walk alone, with a loneliness that we never experienced before the advent of the technological age. Out of this loneliness, this disunity, comes violence and hatred. Where does a farm fit into this scene?

The farm indeed has a very special role. It enables us to touch the earth, to have reverence for the earth, to grow food from it. All this is to be united with God and his creation. As He said in *Genesis*:

> "Be fruitful and multiply; fill the earth and subdue it. Take dominion over the fish of the sea and the birds of the air and over every living thing that moves upon the earth. Behold I have given you every plant-yielding seed which is upon the face of all the earth, and every tree with seed in its fruit; you shall have them for food. And to every beast of the earth, everything that creeps on the earth, everything that has the breath of life, I have given every green plant for food."

He gave us all of this to unite us, but we have misused it very much. We have used everything for profit and for avarice. The big conglomerates have swallowed little farms, and these are signs of disunity, physical and spiritual.

Long ago and far away I dreamt and sensed that a farm, that farming—apostolic farming—could cure these evils that are in our midst and bring about unity through food grown and food shared. It is so simple, so direct and beautiful to share food with those who haven't any; and sharing holds the farmer in its fruits.

If I give a bushel of wheat to someone, into that bushel of wheat went my work, my sweat, perhaps sometimes my tears, for didn't I weep over the weather? That bushel of wheat is part of me, and when one person gives another person that sort of gift, he really gives of himself. Unity is the fruit of such self-giving.

Dorothy Day, foundress of the *Catholic Worker* movement, wrote a lot in the 1930s about "returning to the land." I used to talk with her about it, saying that people who participated in this movement didn't have unity; they were placed on farms because there was no other place for them to go. Dorothy acknowledged that there was bickering amongst them. Father Francis McGoey, who also led a back-to-the-land movement during the Great Depression, had the same experience. And the moment the Second World War came, bringing high wages in factories, everybody abandoned the land. This was not the farming that I dreamt about.

My dream of unity began to be realized

When we purchased our farm, my dream was realized, but I didn't fool myself, for I knew that real honest-to-goodness farmers would come only rarely, and that it was city people with very little knowledge of farming who would come. And so it was. They came from all directions. They didn't know anything about farming but they learned.

What is more, as time went on some of those who became members of our community learned apostolic farming, and my dream of unity began to be realized. Numerous men and women learned about the unity that exists between God and people who work the land. By learning this they became more united with one another. It was beautiful to behold this unity grow.

The food we now eat is more nourishing, more natural

One cannot really be false to God's truth in *Genesis* but, alas, today most farms are. Animals are filled with antibiotics and water for bigger poundage and therefore bigger money. This deception brings sickness, not only of the body—which it does, but also of soul and mind. No farm of ours should ever do that. We can't deceive on our farm. Truth must be the stuff of our farmers' work. It is better, for instance, to let chickens roam around than to coop them in and feed them God-knows-what so that they will produce more eggs. It is better for us to have fewer eggs and be truthful than to have more and be liars before God.

Slowly our farmers began to understand *Genesis*: that we really were given the earth to preserve, and to restore by natural means, rather than polluting it. They have understood that we have to abandon greed and selfishness and avarice. It isn't a question of producing a lot with harmful fertilizers and pesticides. It is a painstaking, almost backbreaking labor of love to make the earth of our farm fertile again by the means with which God meant it to be fertilized.

Gradually our farm is beginning to flower. Many preconceived notions of modern men were shed, and the food we now eat is more nourishing, more natural, and, believe it or not, more unifying, because people who eat the produce of our farmers recognize their labors and bless them, and feel one with them.

Yes, these are things I think about in relation to farming as a unifying entity in our modern world. Let us help to bring small farms back again and do away with huge combines, with lies, greed, and selfishness.

Farming is an altar on which only the bread and wine of truth can be placed.

Part Three

Thoughts from the Farmers
of Madonna House

Ronnie MacDonell:

When Madonna House started farming, all the men were city guys without any experience in farming, except for me. As kids my brothers and I had to run our farm when my father got sick. So I knew what we did there in Cape Breton, Nova Scotia, and I tried to do the same thing here—but the farming conditions were different.

Friends of Madonna House who owned property nearby allowed us to farm their place, and that was our first farm. It included larger acreage for hay, and two and a half acres, full of rocks, for growing vegetables. This was near a swamp, so wouldn't need watering.

We spent one whole summer getting it ready. The rocks were too big to move, so we had to blow them into pieces with dynamite. We would make holes in the rocks, one man holding a chisel while the other would try to hit it with a big maul hammer, to make a crack in the rock. Then we would put dynamite in the crack and blow it up.

To work the soil, we had only hoes and a little motorized plow with handles, that you walk behind. I thought this was ridiculous trying to plow this big field with this little device, and I remembered that we had a small tractor on my family's farm that wasn't being used, so I asked them for it, and it came on the train, together with a wagon. The next year, in the spring, we planted vegetables there.

We began searching for a farm to buy, and found one (the Kelly farm) about six miles from our main house. It wasn't good farm land. One field had rock outcroppings from subsoil boulders, which were impossible to get rid of. For many years the land had been used to grow grain to feed horses which worked at a corundum mine near the farm. Depleted from erosion and overcropping on the steep hillsides, lacking organic content and minerals, the soil lost moisture rapidly, as its base was sand.

It wasn't until very late in the spring, past the ideal time to begin field work, that we arrived at this farm, which was named St. Benedict's Acres. We began plowing the very first day. Soon we realized that we were running out of time, so we started working all night with the tractor, on shifts. How we longed for the dawn to come! We worked all night, and we didn't get much of a break from work during the day.

Before I arrived at Madonna House, Catherine had built a special kind of pig house, designed for pigs having litters. Her pigs were well looked after, and she got top grade and premium price when she sold them. So she was an example to local farmers that it's worth taking care of your pigs properly. We don't raise pigs anymore, though, because we don't have many scraps or waste at Madonna House, and would have to feed them grain. But on our poor soil you can't produce grain very efficiently, so we find that it's better to raise grassland animals, sheep and cows, for meat. Also, Catherine had raised pigs during the warm months only, and constructing adequate winter housing for them would have been too expensive.

Once we men took over running the farm, Catherine would periodically call us to a meeting, usually in conjunction with the kitchen staff. She gave everyone a chance to air their opinion at those meetings. So it felt like a family, with everyone sharing in the development. They were exciting times, really. We had the sense that we were building something for the future, which we couldn't see at all—though we realized that it would take 40 years to rebuild the soil.

During my many years at St. Benedict's farm I was sustained by Catherine's vision of restoring farming to what God meant it to be, to methods that respect and nourish the land. I knew that this was a vital part of restoring the world to Christ. Also I was working to feed the family.

I had always desired to serve in developing countries, and after 33 years at St. Ben's, I was assigned to the Madonna House in Liberia, West Africa, and then in neighboring Ghana. The simplicity of lifestyle, including lifting water from a deep well with a rope and bucket, reminded me of pioneer days at our farm in Canada. There was a shortage of food, because people depended on imported rice to supplement their own crops, and sometimes no rice was available. Almost immediately upon arrival I borrowed a hoe and started to work the soil for a garden. People marveled to see a white man hoeing in the fields.

Since the soil is very poor I got together with some of the young fellows and we planted soil-enrichment crops, including velvet beans. We also begged vegetable and fruit seeds from groups which are working to provide food for all the hungry of the world. A worldwide network of concerned persons is laboring to increase the plant gene pool and to work out systems which allow for good stewardship of the earth and its resources. With the use of organic fertilizer and mulching, crops have increased five times over previous methods.

Albert Osterberger:

I was made farm manager in 1975, and that assignment was a very great blessing for me. Soon after, Catherine began to question me about various aspects of the farm. Albert, why do we do this and why that? She wanted to know everything, and I had to do a lot of research, including trips to our government agricultural representative, in order to answer her questions.

Every year she would give me a project: It's time for you to get set up so we can irrigate our vegetables. It's time to start building a granary because we need to start growing our own grain and start milling our own flour. It's time for you to start learning how to farm with horses.[*] She phoned me from Arizona, where she was visiting the staff in one of our houses: It's time to get a team of bred mares because you have to start farming with horses. It's time to get a windmill. Every year I had a new project.

It was a very demanding and exciting time for me and for the farm staff. Each project that she wanted for the farm struck me as a good idea, and I knew we could do it. All this was formative for each of us.

A number of developments at our farm stand out. First and foremost is the windmill project. At the end of our annual Directors' Meeting in September, Catherine had asked me directly to put up a windmill for our water system. So in November Douglas Guss and I drove to Aylmer, Ontario to pick up a new but old-fashioned water pump windmill system with a forty-foot tower, ten-foot blades, pump, gear box, and so on.

---

[*]   Though we always strive to use our horses in new and creative ways, we do use tractors when it is necessary.

Bill Jakali and I then got together with one of our friends to design a cement reservoir to hold a supply of water for times when the wind is insufficient for pumping. We now have a covered reservoir 33 feet in diameter and 10 feet deep, set into the soil up the hill from our farmhouse and barn. Next spring we still have to pull up the old well pump and erect our windmill tower over the well. God willing, next summer our water supply should be furnished by wind.

Our other new project was a drying building for the herbs that we grow for cooking and medicinal use. Bill and Pat McConville and Charlie Cavanaugh built this small octagonal building that is heated by a wood stove, and made all the shelving and wire mesh drying trays.

We had frost in early June and again in late August. That doesn't leave much growing time and so our vine harvest was nil—almost no squash or cucumbers. We also had no honey harvest at all this year. This has never happened to us before. However our root crops of potatoes, carrots, beets, and turnips were adequate. This is the fourth year in a row that we have not had to travel to beg vegetables from the large growers. In fact we should have lots to share with people in our area who are in need.

From the time that I became farm manager, we started plowing every acre of farm land we had. We plowed every acre of pasture and replanted them because they were so infertile, poor and unproductive. We had been growing weeds and we weren't getting any harvest. Several years later we had finished renewing the pastures on all of our hills and they became quite productive. This was before we got horses. We had to stone every field.

This area was not made for farming. The Department of Agriculture kept telling us that. We would reply that we had to farm to eat. Finally an agricultural professor in Kemptville and a government agricultural representative both said to us, "I know how you can farm this land. You need to consider yourselves grassland farmers, and we'll teach you how."

At that point I asked Ronnie, who was in charge of our animals, to research what kind of horses we should get. In a very short time he said that we should get Percherons. And that we should visit this and that farm in our county which had horses to sell. We started with a team of what we thought were bred mares, although only one was.

We got no foals from our mares that summer but that was probably providential, as it gave Sherman Everson more time training the geldings. Sherman and Larry Klein took a weekend course on draft horses and found it very helpful. Most of our spring and fall field work was done with our horses and for the first time we had two teams working at one time. We bred our mares again and hope to get at least one foal next spring. We had our team shoed for the first time last winter because of the icy conditions. We set up a forecart for a three-horse hitch which Sherman used for the fall plowing. So the horses continue to become more a part of our farm life.

We used our horses more than ever this year. I made a dump cart and Sherman used it for stoning our pastures. The spring seed beds were worked up with the horses and when seeding, we used all five horses, 3 for seeding and 2 for rooling. Larry Klein and Sherman are both good teamsters now, and Scott Eagan is picking it up quickly. He loves working with the horses and is using them in our woodlot preparing firewood. Our farm provides both food and fuel (firewood) for our Madonna House community. Scott and Sherman spread all the farm manure using the horses. The two young geldings are working out but we had some harness break in use, and one serious runaway. No one was hurt nor were the horses. We certainly are protected by Our Lord and Our Lady.

Scott and Sherman had a 5-horse hitch working in our fields. It was a beautiful sight to see five big animals working so quietly and powerfully together! In July a filly was born and Catherine named her Joy. Scott took on her training as soon as she was old enough.

Larry and I fixed up a riding-type horse cultivator, and he laid out the hilled rows of the garden for the first time with a team of horses. We used this device for planting potatoes too. It was the easiest and quickest potato planting "bee" we ever had! We expanded our garden into the drained-swamp area, but we have much to learn before we discover the best way to use this new muck garden soil.

Our grain crop was poor; we had a big problem with weeds. We use no herbicides. We thrashed our dried bean crop for the first time. Fr. Tom Zoeller rebuilt our greenfeeder box and we were able to feed our cattle "green" hay until late fall. Our strawberry, maple syrup, and honey harvests were ample this year. Bill Jakali brought in a good fish harvest from our trout farm which he developed over recent years.

Of some of the things Catherine wanted me to do, eventually I had to say, "We shouldn't do that. I know from our experience as well as from what the Ag Rep said." For example, before I was farm manager she had decided that we should grow corn on this hillside and make our own silo. So we built a silo. We had terrible soil erosion, and also some winter loss with the silage. We never did that again. I learned that we shouldn't annual crop our fields because of erosion; we should do grassland farming.

Larry Klein:

To me, farming is mainly a work of the heart. The real work of the farm is the work of love. The animals, crops, and machinery need constant care and attention. We must conform to them; they will not conform to us. If we expect a machine to behave according to our will, we will break it. It cannot respond to us. We must submit to it.

This is the asceticism or discipline of farming. It is an asceticism of the growing of food, not an asceticism of fasting. To work with an animal is not something we learn from a book. It takes years. As a man said about working oxen: "To work an ox you must learn to think like an ox... but faster!"

However in most cases it seems more a question of working *slower*, of having *patience*. The reality is the same: a man must submit himself to the animal. The animal cannot change. The man must.

We have seminarians who come to our farm as part of their year of spiritual formation. In my heart my word to these wonderful men has been: "Why wait? Give of yourselves. Why are you saving your personal energy resources? Unless you learn to live beyond your energy resources, you will miss something essential. Unless you learn to give of yourself—here, now, today—you may go all through life and never experience the daily joy and happiness of giving full measure of your heart's blood."

It is not a question of working hard or not working. Life requires discipline, yes; but life is primarily a work of the heart, of love. It is a matter of living in such a way that we are *not* living by our own resources, our own discipline. We do not live our own life; Christ lives in us.

We have little chicks at the farm. If the heat lamps go out, they will die. If our attentiveness is not there, they will die, and die quickly. This is the real discipline—a discipline of the Spirit, an absolute and constant listening to the Spirit...

This year our potato crop failed, and we are looking to our friends to help us out. As our foundress, Catherine, says, "Failure is but a stepping stone to success. Farming, like everything else with God, is always starting all over again."

Those who live here, those who come to work with us, and those who come to visit our farm are not the full circle of this farm. We have friends and benefactors who donate peaches, pears, apples, and—this year—potatoes. We are not self-sufficient and do not intend to be. Always, our life and every life comes from the sufficiency of God!

This past year we farmers have recommitted ourselves to providing fresh, wholesome foods, grown with simple methods and great love. We've found that sufficient milk can be produced from our own pastures and hay fields; we don't need to purchase grains in the amounts we once thought necessary. We've been surprised at how well these changes have gone: the cows have less stress and sickness, and still give plenty of milk!

The gardening has changed also. We were able to mulch four acres of gardens with hay that had been rained on. Again, we were surprised at how well they did: fewer potato bugs, and less irrigation and weeding needed.

We realize how much we've had to *un*learn, and how much prayer and death-to-self is required to learn what *is* needed—as we try out simpler ways to care for our gardens and to do intelligent pasturing of our livestock. It was a wonderful revelation to find that the land, even with poor soil, will carry the burden of feeding our large apostolic family, as our farming becomes more permanent and sustainable.

Scott Eagan:

Fall plowing has begun. My partner Greg and I guide our teams of horses over each field and, as we see the soft earth being turned up, many thoughts come to mind.

The harvest is in. Bales of hay are in the barn, stacked in neat rows. The grain is piled in the granary: wheat, oats, barley, buckwheat, hull-less oats for porridge. They are the fruit of our cultivating and seeding almost five months ago. The cows, sheep, and horses show signs of good health and growth provided by the many hillside pastures.

The root cellar is filling up with potatoes...and much more. In a sense, the real harvest is the smiling, healthy, almost radiant faces of the brothers and sisters who will benefit from these products. Despite the drought this summer, with some poor crops, God has provided. We may not have an abundance, but we will have enough to see us through next year.

The harvest is the fruit of our labor, our planning and learning, our listening, our silence, our prayers. God has watched over and blessed this farm. As we continue plowing, surrounded by the splendor of hills in autumn color, it is the land, the earth, that holds my attention.

I reach down and touch the earth. Sandy loam. It is coarse in texture, dark and pungent when wet. Without water, this clump will become a light, sifting mass. There is more than just soil here. There may be a worm or two, a few grain stalks and roots, a bit of clover and grass. Unseen soil creatures, bacteria and fungi add to this complex medium, not to mention the lacework of chemical compounds and organic matter. It is astonishing that a small handful of dirt can hold so much.

Yet what is more simple and ordinary than the earth? You put in a seed; and a little later up comes a sprout, then a plant, then the harvest. It is a given, yet a gift. It is God's good earth. We take it for granted. It has always been there, always will be. Several families have worked these fields before us. We hope to farm this land for many years into the future.

A hundred years from now, will those who farm here inherit a healthy, living earth or one that has been abused, poisoned, made sterile? The answer lies not so much in a philosophy or a technique, but in our relationship with God. The motivation is love—love for God, our brothers and sisters, and all creation.

Our farm is an unusual place. We call it an *apostolic farm*, as our foundress, Catherine, said, "where love spills itself into the earth and gazes at the earth reverently".

This love brings us to see the land as a gift from God. Each piece of earth is an opportunity to love. We begin by sizing up its potentials, by appreciating its limitations, by asking God what we can do to bring nutrition, order and beauty from this piece of land.

Much of our farm is steep hillside. Rocky and sandy, it is poor farmland. If we row-cropped these slopes, we would lose what little topsoil we have. So we keep it in permanent pasture, a valuable crop for our herd. We take great effort to maintain healthy pastures through rotational grazing, weeding, harrowing, and the tons of manure spread in the fall.

When our grain fields become infested with quack grass, we turn to buckwheat and cultivation as the solution, instead of a herbicide. In addition to crowding out the quack grass, the buckwheat gives a low-cost crop useable for feed and flour.

We avoid seeing the land as a mine. We do not just take from the land. We put back in, as the soil and crop demand. We not only fertilize; we try to make fertile.

The difference is in the heart. In looking for ways to work the fields, we employ both modern methods and yesterday's traditions, as love requires. In keeping with the spirit of our Madonna House life, we try to remain simple, poor, childlike. Each day, as we go to the fields to plow or seed or spread manure, we have an opportunity to echo Christ's tenderness for the earth. I have the chance to

bring Christ's tenderness to my fellow work-
ers, to the animals we use, to all living things.

As I cover the ground with my footsteps,
I spread my prayers. I am increasingly aware
that, through my baptism and as partaker of
the Eucharist, I carry Christ into these fields.
He is with me, blessing all his creation and
restoring the land. Each field should speak of
integrity and reflect honesty, for my life is
being spent there. Someone else will inherit
this land, will work it after me. Will it be a
blessing for them? Will it be a pasture or
field or garden worthy of one who carries our
Lord?

The earth is awakening. Farmers are returning to their fields. Here at St. Benedict's—a
farm that pastures dairy and beef cattle, draft
horses, sheep, even chickens—we eagerly
await the day to "go on pasture."

As the hay stocks diminish and as the
brown, seemingly lifeless hillside pastures
ever so slowly awaken, we wait. We farmers
and all the grazing animals wait patiently yet
expectantly. This winter's snow cover has
melted, swelling our little creek. Its waters
flow into the York River, empty into the

Madawaska River, move on into the Ottawa River, and finally into the mighty St. Lawrence and the Atlantic Ocean.

Each day imperceptible growth, much of it beneath the surface, leads to a living carpet. Finally, the day arrives. The pasture is ready! One of the most thrilling sights to a farmer's winter-weary eyes is that day when the gate is opened and the herdsman leads his "beauties" out of the barnyard and up our hill to the first pastures of springtime.

Every animal carries its head high, nostrils straining, heart pounding, its whole attention fixed on that first mouthful of tender spring pasture. A new season has begun. The pastures have come back again!

They are practical, utilitarian, and require upkeep. Work, thought and prayer must be poured into them. The stone fence along the county line has tumbled down in spots. Groundhogs are burrowing holes in the top field. Milkweed and thistles are spreading on "the back forty."

But there is something that feeds the heart there, too. There is a certain beauty and the sense of work well accomplished. A lush stand of trefoil and brome grass that you've seeded and cared for is a beauty to behold. Bobolinks caroling from the old birch tree, which has survived yet another winter, testify to that mysterious schedule of the return of life.

The undulating slope of the land somehow gives peace to the mind. Each pasture is a unique, individual collection of plants, rock piles, and outcroppings, gradients, and memories of work there.

Can a person love a field? Over the years many of us farmers have walked these pastures hundreds, thousands of times to bring down the herd for milking, to walk a fence line, to seed an erosion area. After many years, you know them like the back of your hand. They wear a place in your life, they grow into the heart. And each spring that place in the heart reawakens.

About the Author

Catherine de Hueck Doherty was born into a wealthy family in Russia in 1896. Many different strands of Christianity were woven into the spiritual fabric of her family background, but it was from the liturgy of the Russian Orthodox Church, the living faith of her father and mother, and the earthy piety of the Russian people themselves that Catherine received the powerful spiritual traditions and symbols of the Christian East.

At fifteen Catherine was married to Boris de Hueck. Soon they were swept into the devastating battles of World War I, where she served as a nurse. After the Revolution of 1917 they endured with all the peoples of the Russian Empire the agonies of starvation and civil war. Eventually Catherine and Boris escaped to England. At the beginning of her new life in the West, Catherine accepted the teachings of the Catholic Church, without rejecting the spiritual wealth of her Orthodox heritage.

In 1921 the couple sailed to Canada, where Catherine gave birth to their son George, soon after their arrival in Toronto. As refugees, they experienced dire poverty for a few years but soon Catherine's intelligence, energy, and gift for public speaking brought her to the attention of a large lecture bureau. Her talks were popular all across Canada and the United States. Within a few years, she became an executive with another, international lecture service. She became a North American success story.

In the 1930's, after several years of anguish, Catherine and Boris separated permanently; later the Church annulled their marriage. As devastated as Catherine was, she knew that God wanted something new from her now, but she did not know what it was. The words of Christ haunted her: "Sell all you possess, and give it to the poor, and come, follow Me."

Catherine took a room in a slum section of Toronto and began to quietly love and serve her neighbors, becoming their friend, and praying, hidden in their midst. But when others saw her and heard her speak, they wanted to join her. There was an intensity to her faith and love that lit a flame in the hearts of many men and women. Catherine had not envisaged a community, but when the Archbishop told her that, yes, Christ was calling her to this, she accepted, and soon Friendship House was born.

The works of Friendship House were modest—a shelter for the homeless, meals for the hungry, recreation and books for the young, a newspaper to make known the social teachings of the Church. Catherine initiated an interracial apostolate in Harlem, living with and serving the African-Americans. This work expanded to other cities: Chicago, Washington, D.C., and Portland, Oregon. Friendship House became well known in the American Church.

Catherine shared with her friend, Dorothy Day of the Catholic Worker, the intense struggle to move the Gospel out of books into believers' lives. Even if a few friends, such as the young Thomas Merton, recognized in her the power of the Holy Spirit and an unwavering fidelity to Christ's Church, many others were frightened by her Russian bluntness. Others simply could not grasp the largeness of her vision, especially because her experience of the ways of God were so foreign to them. Finally after a painful difference of opinion over the nature of the Friendship House Apostolate, Catherine found herself pushed again into the chartless waters of the Lord.

This time Catherine did not have to start alone. In 1943 she had married Eddie Doherty, a celebrated newspaperman, after he convinced her and her bishop that he wanted to share and support her vocation. In 1947, then, Catherine and Eddie came to Combermere, a small village northeast of Toronto, where the Bishop of Pembroke had agreed she could work among the rural families.

The community of Madonna House has continued to grow from those early years, and now has foundations or "field houses" throughout the world, including Catherine's native Russia. Her faith vision for the restoration of the Church and culture has inspired many lay and clergy members to live in a unity modeled after the Holy Family in Nazareth. At the main Training Center in Canada, guests throughout the world come to experience and participate in the Gospel life of the community.

As Catherine's inner life deepened and the community matured, she shared the fullness of the inner vocation Christ had formed in her. On the eve of the Second Vatican Council in 1962, Catherine established the West's first poustinia—a desert place of fasting and praying for unity, in, with and through Christ, a unity "that could only be the fruit of love." Her book Poustinia was awarded the prestigious Prix Goncourt of the Academie Français, and has been translated into dozens of languages; it witnesses to her spiritual depth and passionate zeal to pass on her faith in God.

Catherine died in 1985, a woman who had become a spiritual giant by responding to grace.

If you would like to learn more about Catherine Doherty and Madonna House, please visit our website:
www.madonnahouse.org

Books by Catherine Doherty

In the Footprints of Loneliness
In the Furnace of Doubts
On the Cross of Rejection

Madonna House Classics
Poustinia: Encountering God in Silence,
Solitude and Prayer
Sobornost: Unity of Mind, Heart and Soul
Strannik: The Call to the Pilgrimage in the
Footsteps of Christ
Molchanie: The Silence of God
Uródivoi: Holy Fools
Bogoroditza: She Who Gave Birth to God

Available in electronic format at
www.madonnahouse.org/publications

Audio Books
Fragments of My Life, Not Without
Parables, Poustinia, Sobornost, Strannik

Madonna House Publications
Combermere • Ontario • Canada

"Lord, give bread to the hungry, and hunger for you to those who have bread," was a favorite prayer of our foundress, Catherine Doherty. At Madonna House Publications, we strive to satisfy the spiritual hunger for God in our modern world with the Gospel of our Lord Jesus Christ.

Faithful to the teachings of the Catholic Church and its magisterium, Madonna House Publications is a non-profit apostolate dedicated to publishing high quality and easily accessible books, audiobooks, videos and music. Under the patronage of Our Lady of Combermere, we pray our publications will awaken and deepen for you an experience of Jesus' love in the most simple and ordinary facets of everyday life.

Your generosity can help Madonna House Publications provide the poor around the world with editions of important spiritual works containing the enduring wisdom of the Gospel message. If you would like to help, please send your donation to the address below. We also welcome your questions and comments. May God bless you for your participation in this apostolate.

Madonna House Publications
2888 Dafoe Road
Combermere, ON K0J 1L0
Canada
613-756-3728
1-888-703-7110 (toll free)

www.madonnahouse.org/publications
publications@madonnahouse.org